SYDNEY

12/17/98

Dearest Jordan, Fara, Adam. So
To our first overseas guests.
happy we could share a song on
The Bounty and enjoy the surf at
Manly together! Such good memories
to fuck away until our next visit.
Enjoy the book with lots of love and
best wishes for a safe journey home.
David          Ann
         Taylor
                  Ryan

# SYDNEY

## CITY OF SAILS

NEW
HOLLAND

# INTRODUCTION

Sydney — host of the 2000 Olympics — is blessed with a mild climate and one of the world's most beautiful harbourside locations. Australia's largest city and capital of New South Wales, Sydney was where European colonisation of the continent began when Captain Arthur Phillip and the 11 ships of the First Fleet sailed into the harbour on 26 January 1788. From these inauspicious beginnings as a convict settlement, Sydney has grown to become a thriving, cosmopolitan city with a multicultural population of over 3.5 million.

Internationally famed for modern architectural masterpieces such as the Harbour Bridge and Opera House, Sydney has also lovingly restored and preserved its many sandstone buildings which date from the 1800s. Examples of this can be seen in the tourist area of The Rocks and in the gloriously ornate Queen Victoria Building shopping complex. But Sydney has much to offer in the way of natural beauty as well, with the Blue Mountains bordering the city to the west and 60 kilometres of coastline forming the eastern boundary. Australia's two most famous beaches — Bondi and Manly — are both within easy reach of the city centre, and the numerous other beaches, coves and inlets mean that sand, sea and surf form an integral part of most Sydneysiders' lives.

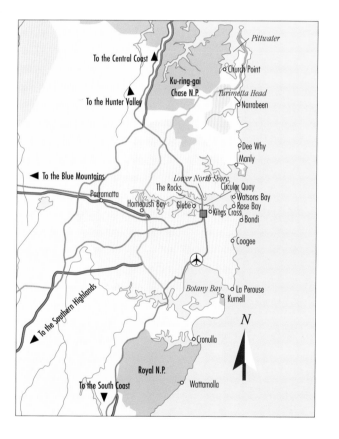

This is a city that knows how to have fun — the Sydney Festival held every January is a vibrant celebration of arts and culture, and March's Gay and Lesbian Mardi Gras attracts visitors from around the world to join in the festivities. Kings Cross and other areas of the city come alive after dark with myriad pubs, restaurants and clubs to suit all tastes and budgets, while Darling Harbour offers 24-hour entertainment for the whole family. Shoppers can browse among the stalls at the popular weekend markets held in The Rocks and Paddington or head for the many upmarket boutiques and complexes along Castlereagh and Pitt streets.

For those in search of a more leisurely pace, Sydney's numerous green areas — including Hyde Park, the Royal Botanic Gardens and Centennial Park — provide ample opportunity to cycle, horseride or simply go for a stroll. To the north of the city, lovers of fine wine can explore the vineyards of the Hunter Valley while, for the more adventurous, a weekend spent in one of the national parks located just outside Sydney is the perfect getaway.

Sydney — ready to meet the challenge of the 21st century — is more than the international gateway to Australia. With its vibrant population, relaxed lifestyle and endless attractions, it is a city every traveller should take time to explore.

Above: Sydney's world-famous Bondi Beach is just a fifteen-minute drive from the city centre.

Right: A helicopter joyflight offers spectacular views of the CBD, Bridge and Opera House.

Above: The Harbour Bridge and the Opera House catch the early morning light as seen from Mrs Macquarie's Chair.

Above: When the Sydney Harbour Bridge was completed in 1932 it was the largest bridge of its kind in the world.

Above: Once a wooded peninsula, then the site of a fortress and later a tram depot, Bennelong Point is now home to the Sydney Opera House.

Above: For a magnificent view of the harbour climb up to the Harbour Bridge pylon lookout.

Following pages: The city glows softly as buildings catch the first pink light of dawn.

Above: Thousands of Sydneysiders enjoy the serenity of catching a ferry to work every day.

Top: Sydney Harbour offers a unique vantage point for some of the best of the city's sights.

Left: Ferries, jetcats and cruise boats all dock at Circular Quay near the historic Rocks district.

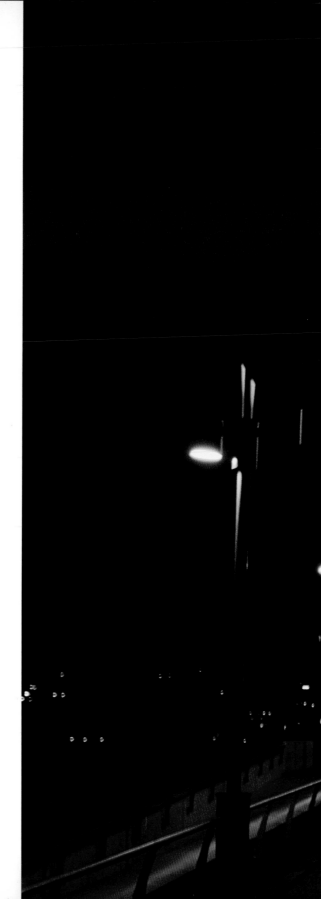

Above: Sydney's superb New Year's Eve fireworks attract hundreds of thousands of spectators.

Right: Luna Park, just over the Harbour Bridge beside Milson's Point,
was once Australia's most popular fun park.

Above: Helicopters, boats and people gather for the start of the Sydney–Hobart Yacht Race, held annually on 26 December.

Left: The myriad spectator craft are almost more impressive than the yachts.

Above: Hundreds of spectator craft jostle with the Tall Ships as Sydney Harbour celebrates Australia Day.

Above: Ferries churn full steam ahead in the Great Ferry Boat Race held during the Festival of Sydney.

Following pages: Refurbished warehouses filled with restaurants line Campbells Cove at The Rocks.

Above: Come aboard the *Bounty* for a harbour cruise into history on the full-size replica of Captain Bligh's original ship.

Opposite: Historic shopfronts line George Street near Circular Quay at The Rocks.

Above: Visitors and locals alike stop for a coffee and a bite to eat, browse amongst the stalls or just enjoy the morning bustle at The Rocks market.

Above: Splashes of colour enliven a wander through the weekend street market at The Rocks.

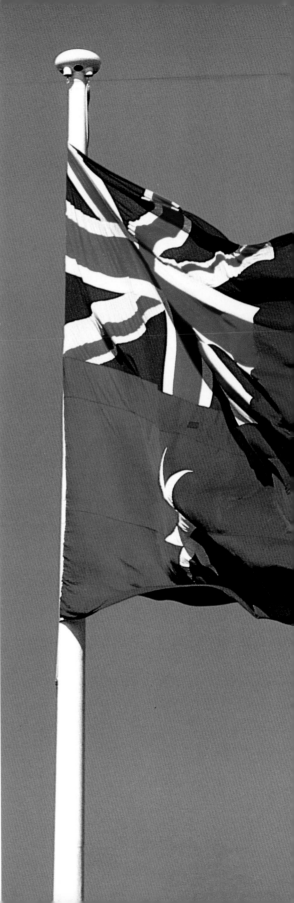

Above: The unusually shaped AMP Tower offers spectacular views of the city.

Right: Changes to the Australian flag are being hotly debated in time for the 2000 Olympics.

Above left: Sydney Town Hall is a fine example of ornate Victorian architecture.

Above right: The delicate spires of St Marys Cathedral rise above the greenery of Hyde Park.

Left: The sandstone edifice of Central Station is only two blocks from Sydney's Chinatown.

Above: The Powerhouse Museum building was once home to the Ultimo Power Station which provided power to Sydney's electric trams until 1963.

Top: The Museum of Contemporary Art occupies the old Maritime Services Board building.

Right: Exhibitions at the Art Gallery of New South Wales attract thousands every year.

Above: Fort Denison, an island in Sydney Harbour, was used as a prison in the early colony.

Top: Built as a convict dormitory in 1819, the Hyde Park Barracks Museum later became a home for destitute women.

Left: The Garrison Church below Observatory Hill in The Rocks was built in 1848.

38       Above: The Queen Victoria Building, replete with copper domes, a barrel-vault skylight and grand entrances, was built in 1898.

Above: Originally home to produce markets, then the City of Sydney Public Library, the building is now a glitzy shopping arcade.

Above: Pier One is one of the Walsh Bay finger wharves just west of the Harbour Bridge.

Left: The Sydney Theatre Company occupies piers Four and Five — a superb theatrical venue.

Above: Horse riding is one of the many activites people enjoy in Centennial Park.

Left: The peaceful ponds of the park were once the source of Sydney's water.

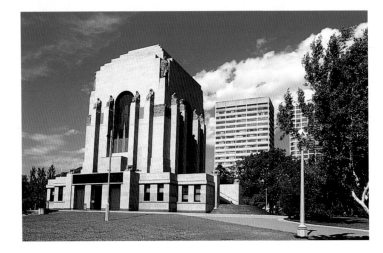

Above: Hyde Park, the site of Sydney's first racecourse, is home to the imposing War Memorial.

Top: Giant chess under giant fig trees attract a ruminative band of players and spectators.

Right: The Archibald Fountain is a beautiful feature of this peaceful inner-city park.

Above: The Pyramid Glasshouse nurtures tropical plants at the Royal Botanical Gardens on Farm Cove near Mrs Macquarie's Chair.

Above: Mrs Macquarie's Chair, named after Governor Macquarie's wife, is the perfect vantage point for the New Year's Eve fireworks display.

Above: Chinese lions guard the entrance to Chinatown's popular Dixon Street.

Left: Chinatown now spreads from Dixon Street through much of the southern business district.

Above: Many restaurants entice hungry passers-by with delicious looking window displays.

Right: The popular Covent Garden Hotel, on the corner of Chinatown's Hay Street, was established in 1910.

50

Above: Bird sculptures soar high above the palms in Darling Harbour's glass-covered atrium.

Left: The Harbourside Marketplace attracts throngs of visitors to food outlets, shops, and bars.

Above: The colourful representation of signalling flags on display spells out the museum's name.

Right: The Australian National Maritime Museum contains sea craft from surfboards to warships.

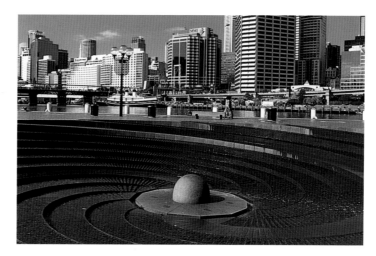

Above: An unusual spiral fountain on the Darling Harbour promenade.

Top: Sydney's monorail swoops from the city across Pyrmont Bridge in just a few minutes.

Left: The Sydney Aquarium displays a large collection of sharks, Australia's notorious crocodiles, dolphins and thousands of native fish species.

Above: Sleek and menacing, a shark slips past Sydney Aquarium's spectacular transparent underwater tunnel.

Above: The pools and willows of the Chinese Gardens at Darling Harbour provide an oasis of calm close to the heart of the city.

Above: Australia hopes for gold in the 2000 Olympics at the Sydney International Aquatic Centre at Homebush Bay.

Right: The morning's catch is put on ice at the Sydney Fish Markets.

Following pages: Blackwattle Bay and Glebe Island Bridge as seen from the Sydney Fish Markets.

Above: The smooth, simple contours of Gladesville Bridge support busy Victoria Road. The tranquil waters of Parramatta River flow underneath.

Above: A charming ferry sight at Birchgrove's Yurulbin Point, just west of the city's centre.

Above: Kings Cross, relatively subdued by day, becomes a hive of activity on Saturday night.

Left: The bright lights of Kings Cross draw people from across the city.

Above: The El Alamein Fountain in Kings Cross is spectacular at night.

Top: Rows of Harley Davidsons are often parked outside the strip clubs of Darlinghurst Road.

Right: A brilliant costume from a Mardi Gras float hits the stage.

Above: Stanley Street in Darlinghurst is a popular inner-city cafe strip.

Top: Taylor Square is the hub of Sydney's annual Gay and Lesbian Mardi Gras festivities.

Left: Paddington streets are lined with 19th century terrace houses, many elegantly restored.

Above: Thousands of people flock to the ever-expanding Paddington Markets on Oxford Street every Saturday.

Above: From brightly coloured flowers and home-made hats to jewellery and artwork, the markets have something for everyone.   73

Above: Bondi Beach is fast becoming the cafe capital of Sydney, but it is still the beach itself that attracts thousands of people looking for a slice of nature in this city of almost four million.

Right: Bondi Pavilion, a thriving community centre, houses pottery and dance classes, a theatre, an art gallery and a musician-in-residence as well as several annual music festivals.

Above: Surf-lifesavers in a rescue boat crest a wave at Bondi Beach.

Top: Two skateboard ramps are situated just off the southern end of the promenade.

Left: Crowds soak up the sun on yet another glorious summer's day at Bondi Beach.

Above: Children, wedged into colourful UV-protection shirts and Legionnaires hats, frolic with their families at Coogee's ocean pool.

Above: Evening falls and the Coogee Bay surf-lifesaving club looks over the now-deserted pool.

Above: Houses crowd the clifftop like lemmings on Ben Buckler, the headland just north of Bondi Beach.

Opposite: The cliffs of The Gap at Watsons Bay, dramatic yet deadly, claimed 120 lives in 1857 when the captain of the *Dunbar* mistook this indentation in South Head for the entrance to the harbour.

Above: The Macquarie Lighthouse on Old South Head Road, the first lighthouse in Australia, is now fully automatic.

Above: Doyle's fish restaurant on the beach at Watsons Bay has been a Sydney icon for decades.

Above: Only the very wealthy can afford harbourside mansions like this one at Rose Bay.

Top: Historic Vaucluse House was the Sydney home of William Charles Wentworth who, with Gregory Blaxland and William Lawson, found a route across the Blue Mountains in 1813.

Right: The rushes of Rushcutters Bay are long gone, replaced by a forest of yacht masts.

Above: A happy visitor to the Koala Park at West Pennant Hills feeds gum leaves to one of the cuddly residents.

Opposite: Taronga Park Zoo, officially opened in 1916, holds over 4000 specimens of vertebrates.

Above: Amenities for animals have been greatly improved since the Zoological Parks Board of NSW took control in 1973.

Above: The zoo occupies a spectacular 32-hectare site overlooking the harbour.

Above: Late afternoon storm clouds darken the sky over a cruise boat at Kirribilli wharf on the Lower North Shore.

Above: An unusual perspective of the Harbour Bridge on the northern foreshore. The stone pylons support over 52 000 tonnes of steel.

Above: The tranquil waters of the harbour beach at Manly are just an isthmus away from the crashing surf of the ocean.

Above left: The busy Corso at Manly runs across the isthmus from ocean beach to harbour.

Above right: Sydney's northern surf beaches are popular with youngsters.

Left: The ferris wheel and merry-go-round at Manly wharf evoke images of English seaside towns.

Above: A brightly painted ferry docks at Palm Beach wharf on Pittwater.

Right: Just across from the heathland expanse of Ku-ring-gai Chase National Park, Church Point is also the gateway to Scotland Island, a bushy suburb in Pittwater accessible only by boat.

Above: A daring windsurfer jumps waves at Palm Beach near Barrenjoey Lighthouse.

Top: Winter surfers brave chilly waters at beautiful Avalon Beach.

Left: Turimetta Beach is tucked into the coast between North Narrabeen Reserve and the dizzy heights of Turimetta Head.

Above: Sydney's northern beaches welcome crowds of surfers and sunseekers every weekend.

Top: Balmoral Beach in Middle Harbour is a popular picnic spot and perfect for paddlers.

Right: One of Sydney's many enthusiastic rock fishermen tries his luck at Manly.

Above: A freshwater stream cuts across the sand at a beach in the Royal National Park.

Top: Cottages clustered above the Park's Little Garie Beach were built during the Depression.

Left: Swimmers at Wattamolla can enjoy the safety of the lagoon or the excitement of the surf.

Above: West Head lookout in Ku-ring-gai Chase National Park offers a magnificent view across the water to Lion Island crouching in the middle of Broken Bay.

Opposite: Barrenjoey Head, north of Palm Beach, is silhouetted against the dawn.

Above: Liberator General San Martin Drive in Ku-ring-gai Chase National Park
hugs Coal and Candle Creek for much of its length.

Left: Coal and Candle Creek is one of many picturesque waterways cutting through the park.

Following pages: Bobbin Head on Cowan Creek is one of the Park's
most popular picnic spots.

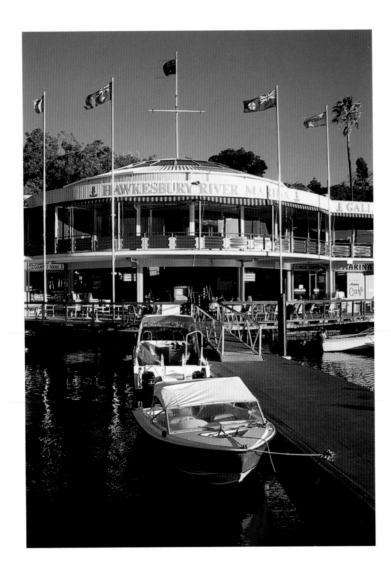

Above and right: Hiring a boat in Brooklyn, on the northern edge of Ku-ring-gai Chase National Park, is a fabulous way of exploring the Hawkesbury River.

Above: This quaint cottage gallery lies on Kangaroo Valley Road south of Sydney.

Top: Hampden Bridge, built across the Kangaroo River in 1898, is the only wooden suspension bridge with castellated sandstone pylons in Australia.

Left: The spectacular Fitzroy Falls in Morton National Park drop a total of 180 metres.

Following pages: The Three Sisters face Mount Solitary across the misty floor of the Jamison Valley.

Above left: Visitors brave the bridge between two of the Three Sisters at Katoomba.

Above right: A tumbling cascade in the Valley of the Waters between Leura and Wentworth Falls.

Left: Late afternoon light warms the sandstone pinnacles of the Three Sisters.

Above: The Hydro Majestic Hotel at Medlow Bath is enjoying a latter-day renaissance.

Top: Once a forgotten mountain community, Leura is now filled with cafes and craft shops.

Left: Autumn leaves cover the ground at Yestergrange, a Victorian house near Wentworth Falls.

Above left: The exhilarating ride on the Katoomba Scenic Railway at Echo Point follows the tracks once used to bring coal up from a seam at the base of the cliffs.

Above right: The Giant Staircase into the Jamison Valley consists of 860 steps straight down.

Right: The Katoomba Scenic Skyway offers breathtaking birds-eye views of the Jamison Valley.

Above: Giant barrels of wine await bottling in a Hunter Valley winery.

Top: Most vineyards in the Hunter Valley, like the Wyndham Estate, offer wine-tasting.

Left: The rich alluvial plains of the Hunter Valley support one
of Australia's quality wine regions.

Above: Dalwood House is an old sandstone homestead on the Wyndham Estate in the Hunter Valley.

Above: Peppers Guest House near Cessnock in the heart of the winegrowing region is just a short walk from Tyrell's famous winery.

Above: Beach umbrellas are a familiar sight at popular Terrigal on the Central Coast.

Right: Families flock to Avoca Beach south of Terrigal for their holidays.

First published in Australia in 1998 by
New Holland Publishers (Australia) Pty Ltd
Sydney • London • Cape Town

14 Aquatic Drive Frenchs Forest NSW 2086 Australia
24 Nutford Place London W1H 6DQ United Kingdom
80 McKenzie Street Cape Town 8001 South Africa

## PHOTOGRAPHIC ACKNOWLEDGEMENTS
Abbreviations: NHIL = New Holland Image Library
Photographic positions: l = left; r = right; t = top; b = bottom
All photographs (c) Shaen Adey/NHIL with the exception of the following:
Vicki Hastrich/NHIL: p. 110; Anthony Johnson/NHIL: pp. 2, 6, 8-9,
12-13, 16, 30, 33 (r), 38, 48, 56, 58, 59, 66, 88, 89 and front cover
flap; NHIL: pp. 50, 121; Nick Rains/NHIL: pp. 4, 10, 17 (b), 24-25,
34 (b), 39, 43, 44 (t), 49, 52, 60, 67, 72, 74 (l), 77 (t & b), 80, 82,
83, 84(t), 95 (l), 99 (b), 100 (t), 102, 112, 113 (b), 116, 117 (l&r),
119 (b), 123 (b), 125, 128.

National Library of Australia
Cataloguing-in-publication data:

Sydney : city of sails
ISBN: 1 86436 375 4

1. Sydney (N.S.W.) - Pictorial works.
2. Sydney (N.S.W.) - Description and travel.

919.44100222

Publishing General Manager: Jane Hazell
Publisher: Averill Chase
Project Coordinator: Emma Wise
Designer: Peta Nugent
Picture Researcher: Bronwyn Rennex
Reproduction: DNL Resourses
Printer: Times, Malaysia

**Half-title page:** *Wild surf at Bondi Beach.*
**Title page:** *Sydney Harbour and the Opera House.*
**Introduction page:** *The Queen Victoria Building and the Coopers
& Lybrand building in the background.*
**This page:** *North Sydney Pool.*